OREMUS

LATIN PRAYERS FOR YOUNG CATHOLICS

introduction by Katie Warner
illustrations after the masters by Meg Whalen

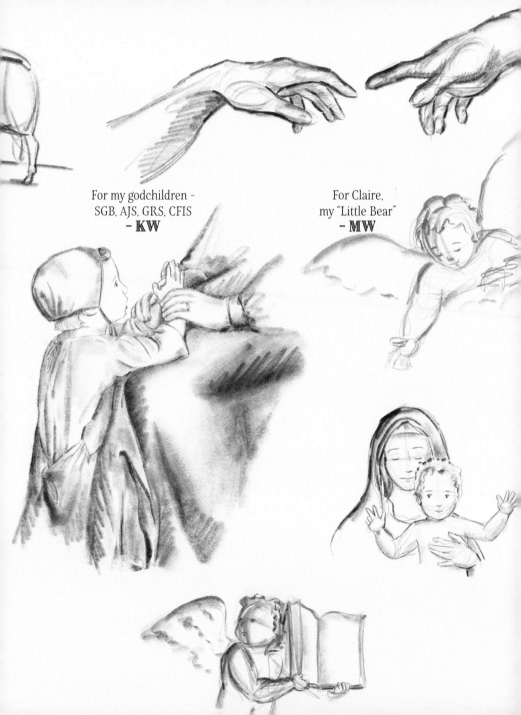

For my godchildren -
SGB, AJS, GRS, CFIS
- KW

For Claire,
my "Little Bear"
- MW

A NOTE TO READERS

"The Roman Church has special obligations towards Latin, the splendid language of ancient Rome, and she must manifest them whenever the occasion presents itself"
(Dominicae cenae, 10).

This book began as an idea to translate our First Faith Treasury board book, *Let Us Pray: A Child's First Book of Prayers* (TAN Books, 2019), into Latin, the official language of the Church. It grew into the beautiful treasury you have in your hands today, thanks to the creative inspiration of the Holy Spirit.

We pray this collection helps children of all ages to fall more in love with the prayers of the Mass and other beloved Catholic prayers, while learning them both in English and in Latin; the language that Pope Saint John Paul II called "an expression of the unity of the Church" and a language which "through its dignified character elicited a profound sense of the Eucharistic Mystery" (*Dominicae cenae*, 10).

In addition to learning sacred prayers in Latin and using this compendium while participating in the liturgy, we want families to become more familiar with some of the great artistic masterpieces that reflect the mysteries of our faith. We hope that Meg Whalen's studies of great master works will draw hearts and souls to the divine in an even deeper way. More practically, we also wish this book to serve as a launching point for exploring religious art and learning the practice of visio divina ("divine seeing"), an ancient form of prayer in which art is used to open one's heart to meditation and conversation with God.

Perhaps your children will further be encouraged to do their own master studies, copying the artwork in their own drawings and paintings, or as a family, you may be inspired to learn more of the history, details, and symbolism behind the pieces chosen for the book (you can find a list of the names and artists in the back).

May this book be a blessing to your family's life of prayer and experience of the Mass, the highest form of prayer! May it help you develop a greater appreciation for the use of Latin in the life of the Church, as well as a greater love for the beauty and spiritual growth that visual art can bring to the faithful.

To God be the glory!
Katie Warner

SIGN OF THE CROSS

In nomine Patris,
et Filii,
et Spiritus Sancti.

Amen.

In the name of the Father,
and of the Son,
and of the Holy Spirit.

Amen.

CONFITEOR

ORDINARY

Confiteor Deo omnipotenti,
et vobis fratres,
quia peccavi nimis
cogitatione, verbo,
opere
et omissione:
mea culpa, mea culpa,
mea maxima culpa.
Ideo precor beatam Mariam
semper Virginem,
omnes Angelos et Sanctos,
et vos, fratres,
orare pro me
ad Dominum Deum nostrum.
Amen.

I confess to almighty God
and to you, my brothers and sisters,
that I have greatly sinned,
in my thoughts and in my words,
in what I have done
and in what I have failed to do,
through my fault, through my fault,
through my most grievous fault;
therefore I ask blessed Mary
ever-Virgin,
all the Angels and Saints,
and you, my brothers and sisters,
to pray for me
to the Lord our God.
Amen.

EXTRAORDINARY

Confiteor Deo omnipotenti,
beatae Mariae semper Virgini,
beato Michaeli Archangelo,
beato Ioanni Baptistae,
sanctis Apostolis Petro et Paulo,
et omnibus Sanctis, et tibi, Pater,
quia peccavi nimis cogitatione,
verbo et opere:
mea culpa, mea culpa,
mea maxima culpa.
Ideo precor beatam Mariam
semper Virginem,
beatum Michaelem Archangelum,
beatum Ioannem Baptistam,
sanctos Apostolos Petrum et Paulum,
et omnes Sanctos, et te, Pater,
orare pro me ad Dominum Deum nostrum.
Amen.

I confess to almighty God,
to blessed Mary ever-Virgin,
to blessed Michael the Archangel,
to blessed John the Baptist,
to the holy apostles Peter and Paul,
and to all the Saints, and to you, Father,
that I have sinned exceedingly
in thought, word, and deed,
through my fault, through my fault, through
my most grievous fault.
Therefore, I beseech blessed Mary
ever-Virgin,
blessed Michael the Archangel,
blessed John the Baptist,
the holy apostles Peter and Paul,
and all the saints, and you, Father,
to pray for me to the Lord our God.
Amen.

KYRIE

V.   Kyrie eleison.   *Lord, have mercy.*
R.   Kyrie eleison.   *Lord, have mercy.*

V.   Christe eleison.   *Christ, have mercy.*
R.   Christe eleison.   *Christ, have mercy.*

V.   Kyrie eleison.   *Lord, have mercy.*
R.   Kyrie eleison.   *Lord, have mercy.*

EXTRAORDINARY

V.   Kyrie eleison.   *Lord, have mercy.*
R.   Kyrie eleison.   *Lord, have mercy.*
V.   Kyrie eleison.   *Lord, have mercy.*

R.   Christe eleison.   *Christ, have mercy.*
V.   Christe eleison.   *Christ, have mercy.*
R.   Christe eleison.   *Christ, have mercy.*

V.   Kyrie eleison.   *Lord, have mercy.*
R.   Kyrie eleison.   *Lord, have mercy.*
V.   Kyrie eleison.   *Lord, have mercy.*

GLORIA

Gloria in excelsis Deo
et in terra pax
hominibus bonae voluntatis.

Glory to God in the highest,
and on earth peace
to people of good will.

Laudamus te, benedicimus te,
adoramus te, glorificamus te,
gratias agimus tibi
propter magnam gloriam tuam,
Domine Deus, Rex caelestis,
Deus Pater omnipotens.

We praise you, we bless you,
we adore you, we glorify you.
We give you thanks
for your great glory,
Lord God, heavenly King,
O God, almighty Father.

Domine Fili unigenite, Iesu Christe,
Domine Deus, Agnus Dei,
Filius Patris,
qui tollis peccata mundi,
miserere nobis;
qui tollis peccata mundi,
suscipe deprecationem nostram.
Qui sedes
ad dexteram Patris,
miserere nobis.

Lord Jesus Christ, only Begotten Son,
Lord God, Lamb of God,
Son of the Father,
You take away the sins of the world
have mercy on us;
You take away the sins of the world,
receive our prayer;
You are seated
at the right hand of the Father:
have mercy on us.

Quoniam tu solus Sanctus,
tu solus Dominus,
tu solus Altissimus,
Iesu Christe,
cum Sancto Spiritu
in gloria Dei Patris.

For you alone are the Holy One,
You alone are the Lord,
You alone are the Most High,
Jesus Christ,
With the Holy Spirit,
in the glory of God the Father.

Amen.

Amen.

NICENE CREED

Credo in unum Deum,	*I believe in one God,*
Patrem omnipotentem,	*the Father almighty,*
factorem caeli et terrae,	*maker of heaven and earth,*
visibilium omnium et invisibilium.	*of all things visible and invisible.*
Et in unum Dominum Iesum Christum,	*I believe in one Lord Jesus Christ,*
Filium Dei unigenitum,	*the Only Begotten Son of God,*
et ex Patre natum, ante omnia saecula.	*born of the Father before all ages.*
Deum de Deo, lumen de lumine,	*God from God, Light from Light,*
Deum verum de Deo vero,	*true God from true God,*
genitum, non factum,	*begotten, not made,*
consubstantialem Patri:	*consubstantial with the Father;*
per quem omnia facta sunt.	*through him all things were made.*
Qui propter nos homines et propter nostram salutem	*For us men and for our salvation*
descendit de caelis.	*he came down from heaven,*
Et incarnatus est de Spiritu Sancto	*and by the Holy Spirit was incarnate*
ex Maria Virgine,	*of the Virgin Mary,*
et homo factus est.	*and became man.*
Crucifixus etiam pro nobis sub Pontio Pilato;	*For our sake he was crucified under Pontius Pilate,*
passus et sepultus est,	*he suffered death and was buried,*
et resurrexit tertia die,	*and rose again on the third day*
secundem Scripturas,	*in accordance with the Scriptures.*
et ascendit in caelum,	*He ascended into heaven*
sedet ad dexteram Patris.	*and is seated at the right hand of the Father.*
Et iterum venturus est cum gloria,	*He will come again in glory*
iudicare vivos et mortuos,	*to judge the living and the dead*
cuius regni non erit finis.	*and his kingdom will have no end.*
Et in Spiritum Sanctum,	*I believe in the Holy Spirit,*
Dominum et vivificantem:	*the Lord, the giver of life,*
qui ex Patre Filioque procedit.	*who proceeds from the Father and the Son,*
Qui cum Patre et Filio simul adoratur et conglorificatur:	*who with the Father and the Son is adored and glorified,*
qui locutus est per prophetas.	*who has spoken through the prophets.*
Et unam, sanctam, catholicam	*I believe in one, holy, catholic*
et apostolicam Ecclesiam.	*and apostolic Church.*
Confiteor unum baptisma	*I confess one baptism*
in remissionem peccatorum.	*for the forgiveness of sins*
Et exspecto resurrectionem mortuorum,	*and I look forward to the resurrection of the dead*
et vitam venturi saeculi.	*and the life of the world to come.*
Amen.	*Amen.*

SANCTUS

Sanctus, Sanctus, Sanctus
Dominus Deus Sabaoth,
Pleni sunt caeli et terra gloria tua.
Hosanna in excelsis.

Benedictus qui venit
in nomine Domini.
Hosanna in excelsis.

Holy, Holy, Holy
Lord God of hosts.
Heaven and earth are full of your glory.
Hosanna in the highest.

Blessed is he who comes
in the name of the Lord.
Hosanna in the highest.

MORTEM TUAM

Mortem tuam annuntiamus,
Domine,
et tuam resurrectionem confitemur,
donec venias.

We proclaim your death,
O Lord,
and profess your resurrection
until you come again.

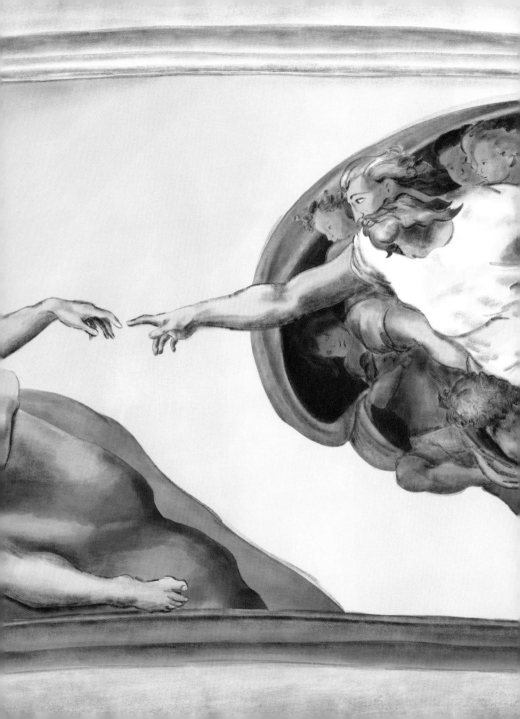

OUR FATHER

Pater noster,
qui es in caelis,
sanctificetur nomen tuum.
Adveniat regnum tuum.
Fiat voluntas tua,
sicut in caelo et in terra.
Panem nostrum quotidianum
da nobis hodie,
et dimitte nobis debita nostra
sicut et nos dimittimus
debitoribus nostris.
Et ne nos inducas in tentationem,
sed libera nos a malo.
Amen,

Our Father,
who art in heaven
hallowed be thy name;
thy kingdom come;
thy will be done
on earth as it is in heaven.
Give us this day
our daily bread
and forgive us our trespasses
as we forgive those
who trespass against us;
and lead us not into temptation,
but deliver us from evil.
Amen.

AGNUS DEI

Agnus Dei,
qui tollis peccata mundi:
miserere nobis.

Lamb of God,
you take away the sins of the world,
have mercy on us.

Agnus Dei,
qui tollis peccata mundi:
miserere nobis.

Lamb of God,
you take away the sins of the world,
have mercy on us.

Agnus Dei,
qui tollis peccata mundi:
dona nobis pacem.

Lamb of God,
you take away the sins of the world,
grant us peace.

DOMINE, NON SUM DIGNUS

Domine, non sum dignus,
ut intres sub tectum meum:
sed tantum dic verbo,
et sanabitur anima mea.

Lord, I am not worthy
that you should enter under my roof,
but only say the word
and my soul shall be healed.

TANTUM ERGO

Tantum ergo Sacramentum
Veneremur cernui:
Et antiquum documentum
Novo cedat ritui:
Praestet fides supplementum
Sensuum defectui.

Genitori, Genitoque
Laus et iubilatio,
Salus, honor, virtus quoque
Sit et benedictio:
Procedenti ab utroque
Compar sit laudatio.

Amen.

Down in adoration falling,
Lo! the sacred Host we hail,
Lo! oe'r ancient forms departing
Newer rites of grace prevail;
Faith for all defects supplying,
Where the feeble senses fail.

To the everlasting Father,
And the Son Who reigns on high
With the Holy Spirit proceeding
Forth from each eternally,
Be salvation, honor blessing,
Might and endless majesty.

Amen.

HAIL MARY

Ave Maria,
Gratia plena,
Dominus tecum.
Benedicta tu in mulieribus,
et benedictus fructus ventris tui,
Iesus.

Hail Mary,
full of Grace,
the Lord is with thee.
Blessed art thou among women,
and blessed is the fruit of thy womb,
Jesus.

Sancta Maria,
Mater Dei,
ora pro nobis peccatoribus, nunc,
et in hora mortis nostrae.

Holy Mary,
Mother of God,
pray for us sinners now,
and at the hour of our death.

Amen.

Amen.

GLORY BE

Gloria Patri,
et Filio,
et Spiritui Sancto.

Glory be to the Father,
and to the Son,
and to the Holy Spirit.

Sicut erat in principio,
et nunc,
et semper,
et in saecula saeculorum.

As it was in the beginning,
is now,
and ever shall be,
world without end.

Amen.

Amen.

SALVE REGINA

Salve Regina,	*Hail, holy Queen,*
Mater misericordiae.	*Mother of mercy,*
Vita, dulcedo,	*Our life, our sweetness*
et spes nostra, salve.	*and our hope.*
Ad te clamamus	*To thee do we cry,*
exsules filii Hevae.	*poor banished children of Eve:*
Ad te Suspiramus,	*to thee do we send up our sighs,*
gementes et flentes	*mourning and weeping*
in hac lacrimarum valle.	*in this valley of tears.*
Eia ergo,	*Turn then,*
Advocata nostra,	*most gracious Advocate,*
illos tuos misericordes oculos	*thine eyes of mercy toward us,*
ad nos converte.	*and after this our exile,*
Et Iesum,	*show unto us*
benedictum fructum ventris tui,	*the blessed fruit of thy womb,*
nobis post hoc exsilium ostende.	*Jesus,*
O clemens,	*O clement,*
O pia,	*O loving,*
O dulcis Virgo Maria.	*O sweet Virgin Mary.*

GRACE BEFORE MEALS

Benedic, Domine, nos
et haec tua dona
quae de tua largitate
sumus sumpturi.
Per Christum Dominum nostrum.

Amen.

Bless us, O Lord,
and these Thy gifts,
which we are about to receive
from Thy bounty,
through Christ our Lord.

Amen.

A NOTE FROM THE ILLUSTRATOR

The practice of making master studies, or copies after master paintings, like the pictures in this book, is one that has been used for centuries. When we talk of these illustrations as copies, we don't mean that we are stealing the work. Credit is always given to the original artist, usually by titling the new picture as "after Raphael" or "after Fra Angelico" and so on.

This practice of copying or studying master works helps us to learn from these artists in a real way, even though we aren't able to learn from them in person. What better way for an artist to improve drawing or painting skills than by drawing or painting the works of the greatest artists who ever lived? And what better way to discover the sacred truths these artists depicted than by studying and recreating the symbols and details the artists included?

Illustrating this book has made me grateful not only to have had the chance to study and draw these master works of sacred art, but also to contemplate, in the details the artist included, the depth and beauty of our Faith.

I sincerely hope that this book inspires you to draw your own master studies as well. It is a wonderful way both to become a better artist and to grow closer to God, the Divine Artist.

On the opposite page, you'll find a list of the original paintings that I used for the prayers. I encourage you to look up these images and learn about the artists who first created them.

May God bless all of you! St. Luke, patron of artists, pray for us!

Meg Whalen

INDEX OF ORIGINALS

A NOTE TO READERS:
Evening Prayer, Pierre Edouard Frère, 19th century
SIGN OF THE CROSS:
Main Apse, Altlerchenfelder Church, Vienna, Karl von Blaas, 19th century
CONFITEOR:
The Prodigal Son, Bartolomé Esteban Murillo, 17th century
KYRIE:
For God So Loved the World, Artist Unknown, 18th century
GLORIA:
The Adoration of the Shepherds, Guido Reni, 17th century
NICENE CREED:
La Disputa, Raphael, 16th century
SANCTUS:
The Entry of Christ into Jerusalem, Félix Louis Leullier, 19th century
MORTEM TUAM:
Messa di Paolo III Farnese, Antonio Maria Panico, 17th century
OUR FATHER:
Creation of Adam, Michelangelo, 16th century
AGNUS DEI:
Adoration of the Mystic Lamb (Ghent Altarpiece), Jan van Eyck, 15th century
DOMINE, NON SUM DIGNUS:
Christ and the Centurion, Paolo Veronese, 16th century
TANTUM ERGO:
The Eucharist Wreathed in Flowers, Jan Anton van der Baren, 17th century
HAIL MARY:
The Annunciation, Fra Angelico, 15th century
GLORY BE:
Holy Trinity, Hendrick van Balen, 17th century
SALVE REGINA:
Queen of the Angels, William-Adolphe Bouguereau, 19th century
GRACE BEFORE MEALS:
Grace Before the Meal, Evert Pieters, 19th century

For more titles from this author/illustrator duo
and resources for forming little disciples,
visit www.FirstFaithTreasury.com.

KATIE WARNER is a homeschooling mom and the author of several bestselling children's books, including *Father Ben Gets Ready for Mass* and *Listening for God: Silence Practice for Little Ones*. She has a graduate degree in Catholic Theology from the Augustine Institute, where she and Meg began their friendship. Katie lives in Georgia with her husband and fellow book-loving children. Find out more about Katie's work, her popular prayer journal series and other books, and connect with her online (she loves to hear from readers!) at KatieWarner.com or @katiewarnercatholic.

MEG WHALEN studied illustration at Rocky Mountain College of Art and Design where she dreamed of making good, true, and beautiful children's books for the New Evangelization. Thanks to her dear friend Katie Warner and their First Faith Treasury series, that dream has become a reality. Meg has a master's degree in Theology from the Augustine Institute in Denver, and she now lives on the east coast of Florida with her husband and children, who are all very cooperative models for many of her book characters. This is her ninth book with Katie.